Why Multi-Generational Teams in Companies Win Faster and Work Better

Why Multi-Generational Teams in Companies Win Faster and Work Better

Tanny Goldsmith

CONTENTS

First Printing, 2026

Part 1: Introduction

The Generational Advantage

"Generational diversity isn't about reducing friction—it's about multiplying intelligence"- **Unknown**

1

Defining Generational Cohorts and Diversity

"In diversity there is beauty and there is strength."
-Maya Angelou

The prevailing narrative around generational differences in the workplace often casts them as sources of friction, communication breakdowns, and management headaches. We're told to brace for clashes between tech-savvy Gen Z and wisdom-rich Baby Boomers, or to mediate the perceived work-life balance demands of Millennials against the steadfast dedication of Gen X.

This perspective, while acknowledging real dynamics, fundamentally misinterprets the most potent force shaping modern organizations.

What if the very diversity that some see as a challenge is, in fact, your greatest untapped strategic asset? What if the generational mix in your conference rooms, on your production floors, and in your virtual meetings represents not a problem to be solved but a competitive weapon waiting to be deployed?

The truth is this: generational diversity is not a problem to be managed, but a profound competitive advantage to be leveraged. When companies intentionally cultivate and integrate the distinct strengths of different age groups—from the disruptive innovation and digital fluency of younger workers to the strategic experience and institutional knowledge of senior employees—they don't just mitigate potential conflict. They unlock a powerful synergy that accelerates business performance and improves organizational outcomes in ways that age-homogeneous teams simply cannot match.

Consider this reality: organizations with high age diversity are demonstrably more innovative, agile, and resilient in the face of rapid market changes. They solve complex problems faster, connect with a wider customer base, and foster a more inclusive culture where every voice contributes to collective success. This isn't about compliance with diversity mandates or checking boxes on HR forms. This is about competitive positioning in an increasingly dynamic global economy where the ability to adapt, innovate, and execute determines who wins and who gets left behind.

The stakes have never been higher. We're living through a period of unprecedented workforce transformation. For the first time in modern history, four distinct generations work side by side, each shaped by radically different formative experiences, each bringing unique capabilities to the table. Baby Boomers who witnessed the moon landing and built careers without email now collaborate with Gen Z employees who've never known a world without smartphones. Gen X professionals who bridged the analog-to-digital transition work alongside Millennials who came of age during the Great Recession and learned to question traditional career paths.

This convergence isn't temporary. It's the new normal.

And the companies that recognize this reality—that embrace it, cultivate it, and strategically leverage it—will outpace, out-innovate, and outlast their competitors who view generational diversity as merely a demographic fact to be tolerated rather than a strategic asset to be maximized.

Think about your own organization for a moment. How many critical decisions are made by teams that span multiple generations? How often do you intentionally pair the pattern recognition of experienced professionals with the fresh perspectives of newer employees? When was the last time your company deliberately structured projects to maximize the complementary strengths that different age groups bring to the table?

If you're like most organizations, the answer is: not often enough.

This insight will guide you through an essential transformation in how you think about, structure, and leverage your multi-generational workforce. We'll move beyond the tired stereotypes and surface-level observations that dominate most discussions of generational differences. Instead, we'll examine the concrete mechanisms by which age-diverse teams create measurable business value—faster innovation cycles, superior problem-solving capabilities, enhanced knowledge retention, and sustainable competitive advantages that compound over time.

You'll discover not just the "why," but the practical "how"—a comprehensive framework for creating generationally intelligent organizations that thrive on the power of their diverse talent.

But first, we need to establish a common language and shared understanding of what we're actually talking about when we discuss generational diversity in the workplace.

Let's cut through the noise and establish clear definitions. When we talk about generational cohorts, we're referring to groups of people born during specific time periods who share formative experiences that shape their values, expectations, and approaches to work. These aren't rigid categories with hard boundaries—someone born in 1964 isn't fundamentally different from someone born in 1965—but they provide useful frameworks for understanding broad patterns in workplace behavior and preferences.

Baby Boomers, born roughly between 1946 and 1964, entered the workforce during an era of economic expansion and relative stability. They witnessed the civil rights movement, the Vietnam War, and Watergate. Many built their careers in organizations that valued loyalty and tenure, climbing corporate ladders that actually existed. They adapted to technology as it arrived—learning to use computers, email, and eventually smartphones as these tools transformed the workplace. Their formative professional experiences often emphasized face-to-face communication, hierarchical structures, and the idea that hard work and dedication would be rewarded with job security and advancement.

Generation X, born between 1965 and 1980, came of age during a period of economic uncertainty and social change. They're the latchkey kids who learned self-reliance early, the generation that witnessed their parents' corporate loyalty. They entered the workforce as technology began its exponential acceleration, making them the bridge generation—comfortable with both analog and digital worlds. Gen X professionals often bring a pragmatic, skeptical approach to work, valuing work-life balance and independence while possessing the adaptability to navigate constant change.

Millennials, born between 1981 and 1996, grew up with technology as an integral part of their lives. They came of age during the dot-com boom and bust, witnessed 9/11 as teenagers or young adults, and entered the workforce during or shortly after the Great Recession. This generation questions traditional hierarchies and career paths, values purpose and meaning in their work, and expects technology to be seamlessly integrated into every aspect of their professional lives. They're often characterized by their comfort with collaboration, their desire for feedback and development, and their willingness to change jobs in pursuit of growth opportunities.

Generation Z, born from 1997 onward, represents the first true digital natives. They've never known a world without the internet, smartphones, or social media. They're entering the workforce during a period of rapid technological disruption, political polarization, and growing awareness of climate change and social justice issues. Gen Z brings an entrepreneurial mindset, comfort with constant connectivity, and expectations for diversity, inclusion, and corporate social responsibility that exceed previous generations. They're pragmatic about career development, having watched Millennials struggle with economic uncertainty.

These descriptions aren't stereotypes to be applied uniformly to every individual within each cohort. They're patterns—tendencies shaped by shared historical moments and technological contexts that influence how different age groups approach work, communication, and problem-solving.

Now, here's what matters for your organization: generational diversity represents a strategic dimension of workplace diversity that's distinct from but complementary to race, gender, and cultural diversity. When we talk about generational diversity, we're referring to the intentional inclusion and integration of multiple age groups within teams, departments, and leadership structures.

This isn't about having a few token representatives from each generation scattered throughout your organization. It's about deliberately constructing teams that combine the complementary strengths of different age groups to achieve outcomes that age-homogeneous teams cannot.

Think of it this way: racial and ethnic diversity brings different cultural perspectives and lived experiences that enhance creativity and market understanding. Gender diversity introduces varied communication styles and approaches to leadership that strengthen decision-making. Generational diversity adds another dimension—temporal perspective. Different age groups bring different relationships with technology, different career stage priorities, different risk tolerances shaped by the economic conditions they've experienced, and different institutional knowledge based on how long they've been in the workforce.

When you combine these dimensions of diversity, you create teams with richer cognitive resources, broader networks, and more comprehensive understanding of both your internal operations and your external markets.

The key distinction is this: while other forms of diversity are increasingly recognized and actively managed in most organizations, generational diversity often remains an afterthought. Companies invest in racial equity initiatives, gender parity programs, and cultural competency training. But how many have deliberate strategies for maximizing the value of their age-diverse workforce?

That's the opportunity—and the competitive gap—we're addressing here.

Generational diversity means more than just having different ages represented in your headcount. It means creating structures, processes, and cultures that actively leverage the distinct capabilities each generation brings. It means recognizing that a 25-year-old software engineer and a 55-year-old project manager don't just have different skill sets—they have different cognitive approaches, different networks, different relationships with risk and change, and different forms of knowledge that, when combined effectively, create something greater than the sum of their individual contributions.

This is the foundation we're building on: generational cohorts are real, their differences are meaningful, and those differences represent strategic assets when properly understood and deployed.

Now, let's deep dive into it by taking the business case in the next chapter.

2

Why Generational Diversity Matters Now

"Stop whining about turnover. Start building teams where a 25-year-old wants to learn from a 55-year-old—and vice versa."-***Unknown***

The Business Case:

The workforce is changing faster than most organizations realize, and the window for strategic response is narrowing.

Right now, approximately 10,000 Baby Boomers retire every single day in the United States. That's not a projection—it's happening as you read this. Each one takes with them decades of institutional knowledge, client relationships, problem-solving experience, and contextual understanding that can't be captured in documentation or databases. The knowledge walking out your door every day represents an invisible but massive drain on organizational capability.

At the same time, Gen Z is entering the workforce in force, bringing digital fluency and technological expectations that many organizations aren't prepared to meet. By 2026, Millennials and Gen Z combined will constitute roughly 75% of the global workforce. If your organization hasn't figured out how to attract, retain, and maximize the potential of these younger cohorts while simultaneously preserving and transferring the expertise of your senior employees, you're already behind.

Here's what the numbers tell us: Companies in the top quartile for age diversity are 45% more likely to report market share growth compared to those in the bottom quartile. They're also 70% more likely to report that they captured a new market in the past year. These aren't marginal differences—they're competitive chasms.

Why? Because age-diverse teams bring cognitive diversity that directly translates to better decision-making and faster innovation. When you put a 28-year-old data scientist in the same room with a 52-year-old operations director, you're not just combining two skill sets. You're combining two different relationships with technology, two different sets of professional networks, two different perspectives on risk, and two different forms of pattern recognition.

The younger employee sees possibilities unconstrained by "how we've always done it." The experienced professional sees potential pitfalls based on market cycles and failed initiatives that the younger employee never witnessed. Together, they arrive at solutions that neither would have reached alone—and they get there faster because they're not repeating historical mistakes or pursuing dead-end innovations.

Consider the case of a mid-sized manufacturing company facing disruption from digital competitors. Their traditional approach to production scheduling, honed over decades, was efficient but inflexible. When market demands shifted rapidly during supply chain disruptions, they couldn't adapt quickly enough. The company formed a cross-generational task force: senior production managers who understood the physical constraints and relationships with suppliers, mid-career engineers who could bridge operational knowledge with technical capabilities, and recent hires who brought experience with AI-driven optimization tools from their university programs.

The result? They developed a hybrid scheduling system that preserved the relationship-based flexibility that senior managers knew was essential while incorporating predictive analytics that younger team members championed. Implementation time was cut in half because experienced employees could anticipate resistance points and navigate organizational politics while younger employees could rapidly prototype and iterate on technical solutions. Within six months, the company reduced inventory costs by 23% while improving on-time delivery rates by 31%.

That's not an isolated success story. It's a pattern that repeats across industries when organizations intentionally leverage generational complementarity.

Or look at the technology sector, where the stereotype suggests youth dominates. Yet the most successful tech companies—the ones that don't just innovate but scale sustainably—deliberately maintain age diversity in their technical teams. They pair junior developers who know the latest frameworks and tools with senior architects who understand system design principles that transcend any particular technology. The junior developers move faster and embrace new approaches more readily. The senior architects prevent costly architectural decisions that would create technical debt or scalability problems down the road.

The financial services industry provides another compelling example. Banks and investment firms with age-diverse client-facing teams consistently outperform those skewed toward either end of the age spectrum. Why? Because their client base spans generations, and clients prefer working with professionals who understand their life stage, communication preferences, and financial priorities. A 30-year-old wealth advisor might excel at explaining cryptocurrency and app-based investing to younger clients, while a 55-year-old advisor brings credibility and experience that reassures clients planning retirement. Firms that can offer both—and facilitate knowledge transfer between them—capture a broader market and deliver better client outcomes.

The competitive pressure is intensifying because markets themselves are becoming more age-diverse. Your customer base includes digital natives who expect seamless mobile experiences and Baby Boomers who value personal relationships and phone conversations. Your competitors include both established players with deep resources and agile startups with nothing to lose. The companies that win are those that can simultaneously innovate like a startup and execute like an established enterprise—and that requires combining the strengths of different generational cohorts.

There's also a talent war dimension to this. The best employees—regardless of age—want to work in environments where they can learn and grow. Younger workers increasingly cite mentorship and development opportunities as top priorities when choosing employers. They want to learn from experienced professionals who can accelerate their growth. At the same time, senior employees report higher engagement and job satisfaction when they have opportunities to mentor and share their expertise. They want to feel that their knowledge matters and will outlast their tenure.

Organizations that create structures for intergenerational collaboration and knowledge transfer become magnets for top talent across all age groups. They're not just filling positions—they're building sustainable competitive advantages through human capital development.

The skill gap crisis adds urgency to this equation. As technology evolves exponentially, the half-life of technical skills shrinks. What you learned five years ago may be obsolete today. But the half-life of judgment, strategic thinking, and relationship-building skills remains long. Organizations need both: the cutting-edge technical capabilities that younger workers often possess and the contextual wisdom that comes from experience. Neither alone is sufficient.

Here's the bottom line: generational diversity isn't a nice-to-have cultural initiative. It's a strategic imperative that directly impacts your ability to innovate, execute, adapt, and compete. The companies that recognize this reality and act on it will pull away from competitors who continue treating age diversity as a demographic fact rather than a strategic asset.

The question isn't whether generational diversity matters. The question is whether your organization will leverage it intentionally or squander it through neglect.

Now, let's learn how to Leverage Generational Complementarity in the next chapter.

3

How to Leverage Generational Complementarity

"Strength lies in differences, not in similarities."
- Stephen R. Covey

Synergistic Strengths

Now we arrive at the core: intentionally combining distinct generational strengths creates synergistic teams that outperform age-homogeneous groups. This isn't about balance or compromise—it's about multiplication. When you properly integrate the capabilities of different age groups, you don't get additive value. You get exponential value.

Let's break down the specific strengths each generational cohort typically brings to the table, and more importantly, how these strengths complement and amplify each other.

Younger workers—primarily Millennials and Gen Z—bring technological fluency that goes beyond mere familiarity with tools. They think in digital terms. They instinctively understand how technology can solve problems because they've never known a world where it couldn't. When faced with a challenge, their first impulse is often to ask: "What tool, app, or platform can address this?" This digital-first mindset drives innovation because it questions assumptions about what's possible.

They also bring fresh perspectives unconstrained by organizational history. They don't know what's "impossible" because they weren't there when previous attempts failed. This can be a liability if it leads to repeating past mistakes, but it's a powerful asset when it challenges outdated assumptions and identifies opportunities that experienced employees have become blind to through familiarity.

Younger employees are often more comfortable with ambiguity and rapid change because it's all they've known. They expect iteration and continuous improvement rather than perfect initial solutions. They're willing to experiment, fail fast, fail early and pivot—an approach that accelerates innovation cycles when properly channeled.

Mid-career professionals—typically Gen X and older Millennials—occupy a sweet spot of capability. They've accumulated enough experience to understand organizational dynamics, industry patterns, and strategic context, but they're still close enough to their early career learning curves to remember what it's like to be new. This makes them natural bridges between junior and senior employees.

They bring strategic experience—the ability to see beyond immediate tactical execution to longer-term implications. They've lived through enough market cycles and organizational changes to recognize patterns and anticipate second-order effects. When a junior employee proposes an innovative solution, mid-career professionals can quickly assess feasibility, identify implementation challenges, and suggest modifications that preserve the core innovation while addressing practical constraints.

They also bring operational wisdom—the accumulated knowledge of how things actually get done in your organization. They know which stakeholders need to be consulted, which processes can be bent and which are rigid, and how to navigate the informal power structures that exist in every company. This knowledge accelerates execution and prevents promising initiatives from dying in bureaucratic quicksand.

Senior employees—primarily Baby Boomers and older Gen X—bring institutional knowledge that's irreplaceable. They've seen your company through multiple strategic pivots, leadership changes, and market disruptions. They understand why certain decisions were made, what was tried before and why it failed, and which organizational capabilities are durable versus temporary.

This historical perspective is invaluable for strategic decision-making. When evaluating a new market opportunity or strategic initiative, senior employees can provide context: "We tried something similar in 2008, and here's what we learned." This doesn't mean they're stuck in the past—it means they can help the organization avoid repeating expensive mistakes while building on previous successes.

They also bring relationship capital—networks of clients, partners, suppliers, and industry contacts built over decades. These relationships often represent your organization's most valuable assets, yet they're rarely captured on balance sheets. When a senior employee can pick up the phone and reach a decision-maker at a key client or partner, that's competitive advantage in action.

Senior employees often bring a longer time horizon to decision-making. They're less susceptible to short-term thinking and more focused on sustainable outcomes because they've seen the consequences of prioritizing quarterly results over long-term health. This perspective balances the urgency and impatience that younger employees bring, creating more robust strategies.

Now here's where the magic happens: these strengths don't just coexist—they actively complement and amplify each other.

When a younger employee's technological fluency combines with a senior employee's institutional knowledge, you get innovation that's both bold and implementable. The younger employee identifies what's technically possible; the senior employee identifies how to make it organizationally viable. Together, they create solutions that are both transformative and executable.

When a mid-career professional's strategic experience bridges the gap between a junior employee's fresh perspective and a senior employee's historical context, you get decisions that are simultaneously innovative and informed by pattern recognition. The junior employee asks "Why not?", the senior employee explains "Here's what happened last time," and the mid-career professional synthesizes these inputs into "Here's how we can do it differently this time."

When a senior employee's relationship capital combines with a younger employee's digital marketing expertise, you get market reach that spans generations. The senior employee opens doors through personal relationships; the younger employee scales the opportunity through digital channels. Together, they access markets that neither could reach alone.

This is complementarity in action—each generation's strengths address the others' blind spots.

Younger workers' comfort with rapid change is balanced by senior employees' emphasis on sustainable practices. Senior employees' risk aversion is balanced by younger workers' willingness to experiment. Mid-career professionals' strategic thinking is enriched by both the fresh perspectives of junior employees and the historical context of senior employees.

The result is teams that are simultaneously innovative and stable, bold and prudent, fast-moving and strategic. They can pivot quickly without losing sight of long-term objectives. They can embrace new technologies without abandoning proven processes. They can challenge conventional wisdom while learning from historical patterns.

This synergy accelerates business performance in measurable ways. Multi-generational teams reach decisions faster because they have more cognitive resources to draw on. They implement more effectively because they can anticipate and address obstacles that homogeneous teams miss. They innovate more successfully because they combine possibility thinking with feasibility assessment from the start rather than discovering constraints after investing in dead-end solutions.

The competitive advantage compounds over time. As multi-generational teams work together, they develop shared mental models that preserve the best of each generation's approach while discarding the limitations. Younger employees learn pattern recognition and strategic thinking faster through exposure to experienced colleagues. Senior employees stay current with technological capabilities and market trends through collaboration with younger colleagues. Mid-career professionals develop both deeper expertise and broader perspective by bridging these worlds.

The organization as a whole becomes more adaptable, more resilient, and more capable of navigating whatever disruptions the market throws at it. Because when you have teams that span generations, you have teams that can simultaneously remember the past, execute in the present, and envision the future.

That's not just a competitive advantage. That's a sustainable competitive advantage—one that's difficult for competitors to replicate because it's built into your organizational DNA rather than dependent on any single product, technology, or market position.

The chapters that follow will show you exactly how this plays out in practice—first, by examining how multi-generational teams drive superior innovation and problem-solving, and then by exploring how they build lasting organizational advantages through knowledge transfer, retention, and culture. You'll see the mechanisms in detail, backed by evidence and illustrated with concrete examples.

But the foundation is this: generational diversity isn't about managing differences. It's about leveraging complementarity to create capabilities that no age-homogeneous team can match.

Part 2: Innovation Through Diversity

Innovation and Problem-Solving Through Diverse Perspectives

"Great things in business are never done by one person. They're done by a team of people."— **Steve Jobs**

4

The Science of Better Solutions

"The illiterate of the 21st century will not be those who cannot read and write, but those who cannot learn, unlearn, and relearn."- ***Alvin Toffler***

Cognitive Diversity:

The human brain is a pattern-recognition machine. We solve problems by matching current situations to patterns we've encountered before, then applying solutions that worked in similar contexts. This is efficient—it allows us to make decisions quickly without analyzing every situation from first principles. But it's also limiting. We can only recognize patterns we've been exposed to, and we tend to favor solutions that fit our existing mental models.

This is where cognitive diversity becomes powerful. When you bring together people with different experiences, different knowledge bases, and different thinking styles, you multiply the patterns available for problem-solving. You increase the likelihood that someone in the group will recognize a relevant pattern that others miss, or will challenge an assumption that's constraining the solution space.

Generational diversity creates cognitive diversity through several mechanisms. Different age groups have been shaped by different technological contexts, which fundamentally alters how they approach problems. Someone who learned to research by going to libraries and using card catalogs thinks differently about information-gathering than someone who grew up with Google. Someone who built their career before email thinks differently about communication and collaboration than someone who's never known a workplace without instant messaging.

These aren't just different preferences—they're different cognitive frameworks. And when you combine them, you get more robust problem-solving.

Consider how different generations approach risk and uncertainty. Younger workers who entered the workforce during or after the Great Recession often have a different relationship with risk than Baby Boomers who built careers during decades of relative economic stability. Gen Z, having watched Millennials struggle with student debt and economic uncertainty, brings yet another perspective on risk tolerance and career security. These different risk orientations aren't right or wrong—they're complementary. When evaluating a strategic decision, having perspectives that span this range produces more thorough risk assessment than a team where everyone shares similar risk tolerance.

The same principle applies to technological adoption. Younger employees often embrace new technologies quickly, seeing potential benefits and being willing to tolerate initial inefficiencies during learning curves. Older employees may be more skeptical, asking harder questions about ROI and implementation challenges. Again, neither approach is superior—but combining them leads to better technology decisions. You avoid both the trap of adopting every shiny new tool without strategic purpose and the trap of clinging to outdated systems past their useful life.

Different career stages also create cognitive diversity. Early-career employees are often focused on learning, growth, and proving themselves. They're willing to put in extra effort and take on challenging projects. Mid-career professionals are often focused on impact and advancement, bringing strategic ambition and operational excellence. Late-career employees may be focused on legacy and knowledge transfer, bringing patience and long-term perspective. When you combine these orientations, you get teams that balance urgency with sustainability, ambition with wisdom, and innovation with stability.

The research backs this up. Teams with high cognitive diversity consistently outperform homogeneous teams on complex problem-solving tasks. They generate more creative solutions, identify more potential risks, and arrive at more robust decisions. The effect is particularly strong for non-routine problems—exactly the kind of challenges that determine competitive success in dynamic markets.

Why? Because complex problems require multiple perspectives to fully understand. A marketing challenge isn't just about creative messaging—it's about understanding customer psychology, competitive positioning, channel dynamics, budget constraints, and organizational capabilities. A team that includes a 26-year-old social media specialist, a 38-year-old brand strategist, and a 54-year-old customer insights director brings different pieces of this puzzle. The social media specialist understands platform algorithms and emerging trends. The brand strategist understands positioning and competitive differentiation. The customer insights director understands long-term customer relationships and lifetime value. Together, they see the full picture in ways that no individual—and no age-homogeneous team—can match.

This cognitive diversity also accelerates learning cycles. When team members bring different knowledge bases, they fill each other's gaps more quickly than homogeneous teams where everyone has similar blind spots. A junior developer who's never worked with legacy systems learns about technical debt and backward compatibility from a senior engineer. A senior engineer who's unfamiliar with modern frameworks learns about new architectural patterns from a junior developer. Both become more capable faster than they would working in age-homogeneous teams.

The mechanism is straightforward: diverse teams have access to more mental models, more patterns, more heuristics, and more knowledge domains. When facing a problem, they can draw on a richer toolkit. They're less likely to get stuck in local optima—solutions that seem good from one perspective but are suboptimal when viewed more broadly. They're more likely to identify creative solutions that combine insights from different domains.

But here's the key: this cognitive diversity only translates into better outcomes when teams have structures and processes that allow different perspectives to be heard and integrated. A multi-generational team where senior members dominate discussions and junior members stay silent doesn't benefit from cognitive diversity. A team where younger members dismiss older colleagues as out-of-touch doesn't benefit either.

The organizations that win are those that create environments where cognitive diversity is actively leveraged—where different perspectives are solicited, where disagreement is productive rather than threatening, and where the goal is synthesis rather than victory for any particular viewpoint.

This requires intentional design. It requires meeting structures that ensure all voices are heard. It requires leaders who can facilitate rather than dominate discussions. It requires psychological safety where people can challenge assumptions without fear of retribution. It requires evaluation criteria that reward collaborative problem-solving rather than individual heroics.

When these conditions are met, cognitive diversity becomes a powerful engine for innovation and problem-solving. Teams don't just solve problems faster—they solve better problems. They identify opportunities that homogeneous teams miss. They anticipate obstacles that would blindside less diverse groups. They create solutions that are more robust, more creative, and more implementable.

This is the foundation of the innovation premium that multi-generational teams deliver. The next section will quantify exactly what that premium looks like in practice.

5

Quantifying Creative Output

"Innovation is taking two things that already exist and putting them together in a new way." - ***Tom Freston***

Let's talk numbers. Because while the theoretical case for multi-generational innovation is compelling, what matters for your business is measurable impact on outcomes that drive competitive advantage.

The innovation premium shows up in three primary areas: patent generation and intellectual property creation, product development cycle times, and market responsiveness. Across all three, age-diverse teams consistently outperform age-homogeneous groups by margins that translate directly to market share and profitability.

Start with patent generation—a concrete, measurable output of innovative thinking. Analysis of patent data across technology companies reveals that teams with high age diversity generate 20-30% more patents per capita than age-homogeneous teams. More importantly, these patents have higher citation rates, suggesting they represent more influential innovations rather than incremental improvements.

Why? Because breakthrough innovations often come from combining existing ideas in novel ways—exactly what multi-generational teams excel at. A senior engineer with deep domain expertise in signal processing might not be familiar with recent advances in machine learning. A junior data scientist with cutting-edge ML skills might not understand the constraints and opportunities in signal processing applications. When they collaborate, they identify opportunities to apply ML techniques to signal processing problems in ways that neither would have conceived independently.

This pattern repeats across industries. In pharmaceutical research, age-diverse teams identify more promising drug candidates and move them through development pipelines more efficiently. In manufacturing, they generate more process innovations that improve both efficiency and quality. In financial services, they develop more successful new products that balance innovation with regulatory compliance and risk management.

Product development cycle times tell a similar story. Companies with intentionally structured multi-generational product teams bring new offerings to market 15-25% faster than competitors with age-homogeneous teams. This isn't because they cut corners—it's because they make better decisions faster and encounter fewer unexpected obstacles during implementation.

Consider a consumer electronics company developing a new smart home device. An age-homogeneous team of young engineers might design a technically sophisticated product with cutting-edge features but overlook usability issues that would frustrate less tech-savvy customers. An age-homogeneous team of experienced engineers might design a reliable, user-friendly product but miss opportunities to incorporate features that younger consumers expect. A multi-generational team designs a product that's both technically advanced and accessible—and they identify potential issues earlier in the development process because they're testing assumptions against a broader range of perspectives.

This early identification of issues is where much of the cycle time advantage comes from. Homogeneous teams often discover problems late in development—during user testing or after launch—requiring expensive redesigns and delays. Diverse teams surface these issues during design and prototyping phases when they're cheaper and faster to address. The senior product manager asks, "How will customers who aren't digital natives interact with this interface?" The junior designer responds, "Good point—let's add these alternative interaction modes." Problem solved before it becomes a crisis.

The cycle time advantage compounds over multiple product generations. Companies that consistently bring products to market faster capture more market share, generate more revenue, and have more resources to invest in the next innovation cycle. Over time, this creates a widening gap between age-diverse innovators and their less diverse competitors.

Market responsiveness—the ability to identify and capitalize on emerging opportunities or respond to competitive threats—represents perhaps the most valuable innovation premium. Multi-generational teams are better at sensing market shifts because they're connected to different customer segments, different information sources, and different professional networks.

When a new competitor enters the market or customer preferences shift, who notices first? Often, it's the employees who are most similar to the affected customer segment. If your entire team is in their 30s, you might miss signals that matter to 50-year-old customers or 22-year-old customers. If your team spans generations, someone is likely to pick up the signal early.

A financial services firm provides a concrete example. Their wealth management division had historically focused on high-net-worth clients approaching retirement—a market they understood well with a sales force and product suite optimized for that demographic. But they were missing the emerging opportunity in younger, tech-savvy investors who wanted digital-first experiences and different product features.

The breakthrough came when they formed a cross-generational product development team. Senior wealth advisors contributed deep understanding of investment principles and client relationship dynamics. Mid-career product managers brought strategic thinking about market positioning and competitive differentiation. Junior team members—some fresh from fintech startups—brought insights about digital user experience and the features that younger investors expected.

The result was a hybrid offering that preserved the personalized advice and sophisticated investment strategies that all clients valued while delivering them through digital channels with the transparency and control that younger clients demanded. Within 18 months, the new offering captured 12% of the under-40 high-income market—a segment the firm had previously struggled to reach. More importantly, it positioned them to grow with these clients as they aged and accumulated wealth, creating a pipeline of future high-net-worth relationships.

The innovation premium also shows up in how companies navigate disruption. When markets shift rapidly—whether due to technological change, regulatory shifts, or competitive dynamics—multi-generational teams adapt more successfully. They can simultaneously preserve core capabilities while embracing necessary changes, a balance that age-homogeneous teams struggle to achieve.

During the rapid shift to remote work triggered by the pandemic, companies with age-diverse leadership teams adapted more effectively. They combined the technological fluency of younger leaders who quickly identified collaboration tools and digital workflows with the organizational wisdom of senior leaders who understood which cultural elements needed to be preserved and how to maintain team cohesion during disruption. Companies that leaned too heavily on either extreme—either embracing every new tool without strategic purpose or clinging to pre-pandemic practices—struggled more and recovered more slowly.

The quantifiable impact extends to commercial success rates. New products developed by multi-generational teams have 30-40% higher success rates in market—meaning they're more likely to achieve revenue targets, gain market acceptance, and generate positive ROI. This isn't surprising given everything we've discussed: these products benefit from more thorough problem definition, more creative solution generation, more rigorous evaluation, and more effective implementation.

Let's look at a manufacturing example. A mid-sized industrial equipment manufacturer faced pressure from low-cost overseas competitors and from high-tech startups offering IoT-enabled smart equipment. Their traditional products were reliable and well-regarded but increasingly seen as outdated. They needed to innovate without abandoning the core reliability that their reputation was built on.

They formed a multi-generational engineering team: senior mechanical engineers who understood the physical stresses and failure modes that decades of field experience had revealed, mid-career electrical engineers who could integrate sensors and connectivity, and junior software engineers who could develop the analytics and user interfaces that customers increasingly expected.

The resulting product line preserved the mechanical robustness that senior engineers insisted on—avoiding the reliability problems that plagued some competitors' smart equipment—while incorporating the connectivity and analytics capabilities that younger engineers championed. The products hit a sweet spot: sophisticated enough to compete with high-tech startups, reliable enough to satisfy conservative industrial customers, and priced competitively because they avoided over-engineering in either direction.

Market response was immediate. Within two years, the new product line captured 23% market share in their core segments and opened new markets among younger facility managers who preferred digital interfaces. Revenue grew 34% while maintaining the profit margins that had been under pressure from low-cost competitors.

These aren't isolated examples. The pattern repeats across industries: multi-generational teams generate more innovations, bring them to market faster, and achieve higher commercial success rates. The innovation premium is real, measurable, and substantial.

But capturing this premium requires more than just having different ages represented on your teams. It requires creating structures and processes that enable effective collaboration across generational lines—which brings us to the practical mechanisms for bridging communication gaps and maximizing cross-generational synergy.

In the next chapter, let's learn how to bring collaboration among a multi-generational team.

6

Bridging Communication Gaps

*"To win in the marketplace, you must first win in the workplace."- **Doug Conant***

Cross-Generational Collaboration

Let's acknowledge the elephant in the room: multi-generational teams aren't automatically effective. Put a 24-year-old and a 58-year-old in a room together, and they don't automatically collaborate brilliantly. They might struggle to communicate. They might make assumptions about each other based on stereotypes. They might have different work styles that create friction rather than synergy.

The innovation premium we've been discussing doesn't happen by accident. It happens when organizations intentionally create structures, processes, and cultural norms that enable effective cross-generational collaboration.

The good news? The barriers to effective multi-generational collaboration are well-understood and addressable. The companies that excel at leveraging generational diversity have figured out how to bridge communication gaps, align different work styles, and create environments where age becomes an asset rather than a source of friction.

Start with communication—the most commonly cited challenge in multi-generational teams. Different generations have different communication preferences shaped by the technologies they grew up with. Baby Boomers often prefer phone calls or face-to-face meetings for important discussions. Gen X tends to be comfortable with email and direct communication. Millennials often prefer instant messaging and collaborative platforms. Gen Z expects seamless integration across multiple channels and is comfortable with video communication.

These aren't just preferences—they reflect different assumptions about what constitutes effective communication. Older employees often view a phone call as more personal and effective than an email, while younger employees might see an unexpected phone call as intrusive and inefficient when a quick message would suffice. Younger employees might interpret delayed email responses as disinterest, while older employees might see immediate responses as indicating someone isn't focused on deep work.

The solution isn't to force everyone to adopt a single communication style. It's to create explicit norms about which channels are appropriate for which purposes, and to build flexibility into how team members interact.

High-performing multi-generational teams establish communication protocols that respect different preferences while ensuring everyone stays informed. They might agree that urgent issues warrant phone calls or instant messages, that project updates go through a shared platform everyone checks regularly, that strategic discussions happen in scheduled meetings where everyone can prepare, and that informal collaboration can happen through whatever channels work best for the people involved.

They also build in redundancy—important information gets communicated through multiple channels to ensure it reaches everyone. A project update might be posted in a shared workspace, summarized in an email, and discussed briefly in a team meeting. This feels inefficient, but it's actually more efficient than having team members miss critical information because it was only communicated through a channel they don't monitor closely.

The key is making these protocols explicit rather than assuming everyone shares the same communication norms. When a team takes 30 minutes to discuss and document how they'll communicate, they prevent hours of frustration and miscommunication down the road.

Mentorship structures represent another powerful mechanism for bridging generational gaps while accelerating knowledge transfer. Traditional mentorship—where senior employees guide junior employees—remains valuable. But the most effective multi-generational teams also implement reverse mentoring, where younger employees mentor senior employees on new technologies, emerging trends, and changing market dynamics.

Reverse mentoring serves multiple purposes. It accelerates senior employees' learning about technologies and trends they need to understand. It gives junior employees visibility and voice, making them feel valued and heard. It breaks down hierarchical barriers and creates relationships that facilitate collaboration. And it forces both parties to articulate their knowledge explicitly, which deepens understanding for both mentor and mentee.

A global consulting firm implemented a formal reverse mentoring program pairing junior consultants with senior partners. Junior consultants mentored partners on social media, digital marketing, and emerging technologies. Partners mentored junior consultants on client relationship management, strategic thinking, and business development. Both groups reported that the experience was transformative—not just for the knowledge transferred, but for the relationships built and the mutual respect developed.

The program had unexpected benefits. Partners became more effective at winning business with younger client decision-makers because they understood the digital channels and communication styles these clients preferred. Junior consultants developed strategic thinking skills faster because they had regular access to senior partners who could explain the reasoning behind high-stakes decisions. And the firm's culture shifted—age-based assumptions diminished as people worked together across generational lines.

Structured collaboration frameworks provide another mechanism for maximizing multi-generational effectiveness. These frameworks create processes that ensure diverse perspectives are heard and integrated rather than allowing dominant voices—whether based on seniority, confidence, or communication style—to overwhelm others.

One effective approach is the "round-robin" discussion format where everyone contributes before open discussion begins. When facing a problem or decision, the team leader asks each person to share their perspective in turn. This ensures that junior team members speak before they've heard senior members' views, preventing the common dynamic where younger employees simply agree with whatever senior employees say first. It also ensures that quieter team members contribute, regardless of age.

Another approach is "pre-mortem" analysis where teams imagine a project has failed and work backward to identify what went wrong. This technique is particularly effective for multi-generational teams because it allows different perspectives to surface potential risks without anyone feeling like they're being negative or challenging authority. A junior employee might identify a technology risk that senior employees weren't aware of. A senior employee might identify a political or organizational risk that junior employees didn't anticipate. By framing these as hypothetical future problems rather than current criticisms, the technique makes it psychologically safe to voice concerns.

"Innovation sprints" or "design thinking" workshops provide structured processes for collaborative problem-solving that level the playing field across generations. These approaches emphasize rapid ideation, prototyping, and testing rather than lengthy analysis and debate. They create space for different thinking styles to contribute—the divergent thinking that younger employees often excel at during ideation phases, and the convergent thinking that experienced employees bring during evaluation and refinement phases.

Technology platforms can also facilitate cross-generational collaboration when implemented thoughtfully. Shared workspaces, project management tools, and collaborative documents create transparency and shared context that helps bridge communication gaps. Everyone can see project status, decisions, and discussions regardless of when or how they prefer to work.

But—and this is important—technology only helps if everyone is trained and supported in using it. Rolling out a new collaboration platform and expecting everyone to figure it out themselves creates a new source of generational friction. Younger employees adapt quickly while older employees struggle, leading to a two-tier system where some people are in the loop and others aren't.

Effective implementations include training tailored to different skill levels, ongoing support, and patience during adoption periods. They also involve younger employees in teaching older colleagues—another form of reverse mentoring that builds relationships while transferring knowledge.

Team composition matters too. The most effective multigenerational teams aren't just diverse—they're balanced. A team with one junior employee and five senior employees doesn't benefit much from generational diversity because the junior employee's perspective gets overwhelmed. Similarly, a team with one senior employee and five junior employees misses much of the potential benefit because the senior employee's knowledge doesn't get fully integrated.

Research suggests that the sweet spot is roughly balanced representation—not necessarily equal numbers, but enough of each generation that no one feels like a token representative. When team members see others from their generation, they're more likely to speak up and contribute fully. When each generation has critical mass, the team develops norms that respect all perspectives rather than defaulting to the preferences of the dominant group.

The role of team leaders is crucial in multi-generational teams. Effective leaders actively facilitate cross-generational collaboration rather than simply assembling diverse teams and hoping synergy emerges. They model respect for different perspectives. They intervene when generational stereotypes surface. They create structures that ensure all voices are heard. They recognize and reward collaborative behavior rather than individual heroics.

They also help team members understand each other's contexts. When a senior employee seems resistant to a new technology, the leader might explain the history of previous technology implementations that failed, helping younger employees understand that the resistance isn't about being stuck in the past—it's about learned caution based on experience. When a junior employee seems impatient with established processes, the leader might explain the regulatory or risk management reasons those processes exist, helping the junior employee understand that the processes aren't arbitrary bureaucracy—they're protective measures based on past problems.

This contextual understanding transforms potential friction into productive dialogue. Instead of "You're being resistant to change" versus "You're being reckless," the conversation becomes "How do we innovate while managing the risks you've identified?" That's a solvable problem.

Psychological safety—the belief that you can speak up, ask questions, and make mistakes without being punished or humiliated—is particularly important in multi-generational teams. Junior employees need to feel safe challenging senior employees' assumptions. Senior employees need to feel safe admitting when they don't understand something. Everyone needs to feel safe saying "I don't know" or "I was wrong."

Leaders create psychological safety through their own behavior—admitting their own mistakes, asking questions, responding constructively to challenges—and through how they respond when others take interpersonal risks. When a junior employee challenges a senior employee's idea and the leader responds with curiosity rather than defensiveness, they signal that such challenges are welcome. When a senior employee admits they don't understand a new technology and the leader treats it as a learning opportunity rather than a weakness, they signal that vulnerability is acceptable.

The payoff for getting this right is substantial. Teams that successfully bridge generational communication gaps don't just avoid friction—they create environments where cognitive diversity translates into better outcomes. They solve problems faster because they can tap into diverse knowledge bases without communication overhead slowing them down. They innovate more effectively because different perspectives are integrated rather than siloed. They execute more successfully because they've identified and addressed potential obstacles that homogeneous teams would miss.

And they create something else that's valuable: they help team members grow. Junior employees in effective multi-generational teams develop strategic thinking and judgment faster because they're learning from experienced colleagues. Senior employees stay current and relevant because they're learning from younger colleagues. Everyone becomes more adaptable, more capable, and more valuable.

This learning and growth creates a virtuous cycle. As team members develop cross-generational collaboration skills, they become more effective in future multi-generational teams. As organizations build cultures that value and leverage generational diversity, they attract talent across all age groups who want to work in such environments. As multi-generational collaboration becomes normalized rather than exceptional, the barriers diminish and the benefits compound.

The companies that master cross-generational collaboration don't just capture the innovation premium we discussed earlier. They build sustainable competitive advantages that extend far beyond any single product or market cycle—which is exactly what we'll explore in the next section.

Part 3: Sustainable Advantage

Building Sustainable Competitive Advantage

"When people are financially invested, they want a return. When people are emotionally invested, they want to contribute."- **Simon Sinek**

7

Intergenerational Knowledge Transfer

"Knowledge doesn't transfer in databases. It transfers in relationships." - ***Unknown***

Every day, critical knowledge walks out your door. Sometimes it leaves when employees retire. Sometimes it leaves when they change jobs. Sometimes it simply fades as people forget details that seemed unimportant at the time but turn out to matter later.

This knowledge loss is invisible on balance sheets, but its impact is real and costly. When an experienced employee leaves, they take with them not just their technical skills—which can be replaced by hiring someone with similar credentials—but their contextual knowledge, their understanding of why things are the way they are, their network of relationships, and their accumulated wisdom about what works and what doesn't in your specific organizational context.

You can't capture this knowledge in documentation. You can't preserve it in databases. The only way to prevent it from walking out the door is to transfer it to other people before it leaves—and the most effective mechanism for that transfer is intergenerational collaboration.

Multi-generational teams create natural knowledge transfer systems. When a 28-year-old and a 56-year-old work together on projects, knowledge flows in both directions. The younger employee learns not just technical skills but judgment—how to assess situations, how to navigate organizational dynamics, how to identify which details matter and which don't. The older employee stays current with new technologies and approaches, maintaining their relevance and effectiveness.

This transfer happens through daily interactions, not formal training programs. It happens when the experienced employee explains why a particular approach won't work based on a failed initiative from five years ago. It happens when the junior employee shows the senior employee a new tool that solves a problem they've been working around for years. It happens in the questions asked, the decisions explained, and the problems solved together.

The cumulative effect is organizational resilience—the ability to maintain capability and performance even as individual employees come and go. When knowledge is distributed across multiple generations rather than concentrated in a single age cohort, the organization isn't vulnerable to sudden capability loss when that cohort retires.

Consider the aerospace industry, where product development cycles span decades and institutional knowledge is particularly valuable. A commercial aircraft program might run for 30 years from initial design through production and support. Engineers who worked on early design decisions need to transfer their knowledge to engineers who will support the aircraft 20 years later when the original designers have retired.

Companies that excel at this create intentional overlaps—they bring junior engineers onto programs years before senior engineers retire, creating extended periods of collaboration where knowledge transfer happens organically. They structure projects so that experienced and early-career engineers work together on complex problems, not just having senior engineers review junior engineers' work but actually collaborating on solutions.

The companies that don't do this well face recurring crises. A critical system fails, and the engineer who understood its quirks retired three years ago. A customer has a unique requirement, and the sales executive who managed that relationship for 20 years is gone. A manufacturing process produces defects, and the production manager who knew how to troubleshoot it left last year.

Each crisis is solvable—you can hire consultants, reverse-engineer solutions, or rebuild relationships—but it's expensive and time-consuming. And the cumulative effect of repeated knowledge loss is organizational amnesia, where the company keeps relearning the same lessons because institutional memory doesn't persist across generations.

The financial impact is substantial. When you lose an experienced employee and have to replace them with someone new, the direct costs include recruitment, onboarding, and the productivity gap during the new employee's learning curve. But the indirect costs—the lost institutional knowledge, the repeated mistakes, the missed opportunities—often exceed the direct costs by multiples.

Conversely, when you successfully transfer knowledge across generations, you get compound returns. The junior employee who learns from a senior mentor becomes more productive faster than they would through independent learning. They avoid mistakes that would have cost time and money. They build on existing knowledge rather than starting from scratch. And eventually, they become the senior employee who mentors the next generation, creating a continuous cycle of knowledge preservation and enhancement.

This knowledge transfer also enables innovation in ways that aren't immediately obvious. When junior employees understand the historical context and accumulated wisdom that senior employees possess, they can innovate more effectively. They can distinguish between constraints that are fundamental and constraints that are historical artifacts. They can build on previous successes rather than reinventing wheels. They can avoid dead ends that previous generations already explored.

A pharmaceutical company provides a concrete example. Drug development is a long, expensive process where institutional knowledge is invaluable. Experienced researchers understand which molecular structures are likely to have problematic side effects, which development pathways tend to encounter regulatory obstacles, and which therapeutic approaches have been tried and failed in the past.

When this company structured their research teams to pair experienced scientists with early-career researchers, they saw measurable improvements in development efficiency. Junior researchers brought fresh perspectives and familiarity with new techniques. Senior researchers provided context that helped focus efforts on promising directions. The combination reduced the time and cost of bringing new drugs through development pipelines.

More importantly, the knowledge transfer was bidirectional. Senior researchers learned new techniques and approaches from junior colleagues, keeping their skills current. Junior researchers learned judgment and strategic thinking from senior colleagues, accelerating their development into independent researchers. Both groups became more capable, and the organization's overall research capability increased rather than simply maintaining steady state as people retired and were replaced.

The succession planning benefits are equally important. When knowledge transfer happens continuously through multi-generational collaboration, succession becomes smooth rather than traumatic. The person stepping into a senior role has already been learning from their predecessor for years. They understand not just the technical requirements but the relationships, the context, and the judgment required for the role.

Contrast this with organizations where succession planning is an afterthought. A senior leader announces retirement, and the organization scrambles to identify a replacement. The replacement steps into the role with incomplete knowledge, learning through trial and error while the organization suffers through the transition. Critical relationships lapse. Important context is lost. Momentum stalls.

Multi-generational teams prevent this scenario by making succession planning continuous rather than episodic. At any given time, multiple people understand each critical role well enough to step into it if needed. Knowledge isn't concentrated in single individuals—it's distributed across the team. This creates both resilience and flexibility.

The cultural impact extends beyond knowledge preservation. When organizations prioritize intergenerational knowledge transfer, they signal that experience is valued, that learning is continuous, and that everyone has something to contribute regardless of age. This creates a culture of mutual respect and continuous improvement that attracts and retains talent across all generations.

Junior employees want to work in organizations where they can learn from experienced colleagues who are willing to mentor them. Senior employees want to work in organizations where their knowledge is valued and where they have opportunities to make lasting contributions by developing the next generation. When both groups find what they're looking for, engagement and retention improve—which brings us to the next mechanism of sustainable competitive advantage.

Now, let's explore business case studies on retention, engagement, and turnover economics in the next chapter.

8

Retention Engagement and Turnover Economics

"People work for money but go the extra mile for recognition, praise, and rewards."- ***Dale Carnegie***

The Business Case:

Turnover is expensive. Every time an employee leaves, you incur direct costs—recruitment, hiring, onboarding—and indirect costs—lost productivity, disrupted relationships, reduced team effectiveness. For professional roles, the total cost of turnover typically ranges from 50% to 200% of annual salary. For senior roles with specialized knowledge, the cost can be even higher.

Now multiply that by the number of employees who leave each year, and you're looking at a substantial drag on organizational performance and profitability. Even a modest reduction in turnover translates directly to bottom-line improvement.

Multi-generational teams reduce turnover through multiple mechanisms, creating a retention advantage that compounds over time.

Start with engagement—the degree to which employees are committed to their work and their organization. Engaged employees are more productive, more innovative, and less likely to leave. And engagement is strongly influenced by whether employees feel valued, whether they're learning and growing, and whether they see a future for themselves in the organization.

Multi-generational teams enhance engagement for all age groups, but through different mechanisms for each generation.

Junior employees report higher engagement when they have access to mentorship and development opportunities. They want to learn from experienced colleagues who can accelerate their growth. When they work in multi-generational teams where such mentorship is available, they're more likely to stay because they're developing faster than they would elsewhere. The organization becomes a place where they're building their careers, not just collecting paychecks.

Mid-career employees report higher engagement when they have opportunities to make meaningful impact and advance their careers. Multi-generational teams provide both. They can mentor junior employees, which is intrinsically rewarding and develops leadership skills. They can learn from senior employees, which helps them prepare for more senior roles. And they can contribute their strategic and operational expertise to high-impact projects. All of this creates a sense of purpose and progress that drives engagement.

Senior employees report higher engagement when they feel their experience is valued and when they have opportunities to leave a legacy. Multi-generational teams provide exactly this. When senior employees mentor younger colleagues, they're not just transferring knowledge—they're making lasting contributions that will outlive their tenure. When their expertise is actively sought and integrated into important decisions, they feel valued rather than sidelined. This sense of purpose and respect drives engagement even as employees approach retirement.

The data backs this up. Organizations with high generational diversity report engagement scores 15-20% higher than those with low diversity. More importantly, engagement scores are higher across all age groups, not just for the groups that are well-represented. This suggests that generational diversity creates a rising tide that lifts all boats—a culture where everyone feels valued and engaged regardless of age.

Higher engagement translates directly to lower turnover. Engaged employees are less likely to leave, both because they're satisfied with their current situation and because they see a future for themselves in the organization. When you reduce turnover, you reduce costs and improve organizational capability.

But the retention benefits go beyond engagement. Multi-generational teams also create social bonds that make people less likely to leave. When you work closely with colleagues across generations, you develop relationships that are both professionally valuable and personally meaningful. These relationships create organizational attachment that transcends any particular role or project.

A junior employee might stay with an organization because they have a mentor who's invested in their development and who they don't want to disappoint. A senior employee might delay retirement because they're engaged in mentoring relationships that give them purpose and satisfaction. A mid-career employee might turn down an external offer because they value the learning opportunities and relationships they have in their current multi-generational team.

These social bonds are particularly powerful because they're not easily replicated. A competitor can offer higher salary or better benefits, but they can't replicate the specific relationships and team dynamics that an employee has built over years of collaboration. This creates switching costs that reduce turnover.

The economic impact is substantial. Consider an organization with 1,000 employees and 15% annual turnover—typical for many industries. If average turnover cost is 75% of salary and average salary is $75,000, annual turnover cost is approximately $8.4 million. If multi-generational team structures reduce turnover by just 3 percentage points—a conservative estimate based on engagement data—the annual savings exceed $1.6 million. Over five years, that's $8 million in direct savings, not counting the productivity and capability benefits of having more experienced, stable teams.

The retention advantage also creates a virtuous cycle. When turnover is lower, teams are more stable. When teams are more stable, they're more effective because members have worked together longer and developed better collaboration patterns. When teams are more effective, engagement increases. When engagement increases, turnover decreases further. The cycle reinforces itself.

This stability also enables longer-term thinking and planning. When you're not constantly backfilling positions and onboarding new employees, you can focus on development, improvement, and innovation. When team members know they'll be working together for years rather than months, they invest more in relationships and shared understanding. When institutional knowledge is preserved rather than constantly walking out the door, the organization can build on its capabilities rather than just maintaining them.

The competitive advantage extends to talent acquisition. Organizations known for strong multi-generational cultures and low turnover become talent magnets. They attract candidates across all age groups who want to work in environments where they can learn, grow, and make lasting contributions.

Junior candidates are attracted by mentorship and development opportunities. They want to work with experienced professionals who can accelerate their growth. Mid-career candidates are attracted by the opportunity to work in high-performing teams and develop leadership skills. Senior candidates are attracted by cultures that value experience and provide opportunities for meaningful contribution.

This talent attraction advantage compounds the retention advantage. When you're attracting better candidates, you're hiring people who are more likely to succeed and stay. When you're hiring people who are more likely to stay, you're building more stable, capable teams. When you have more stable, capable teams, you become even more attractive to top talent.

The employer branding benefits are real and measurable. Organizations with strong reputations for generational diversity and inclusion receive more applications per opening, attract higher-quality candidates, and have higher offer acceptance rates. They spend less on recruitment because candidates seek them out rather than needing to be actively recruited. And they get better hiring outcomes because they're selecting from larger, stronger candidate pools.

All of this translates to competitive advantage that's difficult for competitors to replicate. You can copy a competitor's product or strategy relatively quickly. You can't quickly replicate a culture of engagement, retention, and continuous development that's been built over years through intentional multi-generational team structures.

This is sustainable competitive advantage—advantage that persists because it's embedded in organizational capabilities and culture rather than dependent on any particular product, technology, or market position. And its advantage that compounds over time as the benefits of retention, engagement, and talent attraction reinforce each other.

But capturing these benefits requires intentional design and implementation—which brings us to the practical framework for creating generationally intelligent organizations.

Now, let's learn about creating generationally intelligent organizations in the next chapter.

9

Creating Generationally Intelligent Organizations

*"Nothing will work unless you do," - **Warren Bennis***

Implementation Framework:

Understanding why multi-generational teams create competitive advantage is one thing. Actually building an organization that captures this advantage is another. The gap between theory and practice is where most diversity initiatives fail—not because the theory is wrong, but because implementation is hard and requires sustained commitment and thoughtful design.

This section provides a practical framework for creating generationally intelligent organizations—companies that don't just tolerate age diversity but actively leverage it as a strategic asset. This framework addresses hiring practices, team composition, leadership development, cultural initiatives, and the systems and processes that enable effective cross-generational collaboration.

Start with intentional hiring practices. Most organizations hire for specific roles with specific requirements, paying little attention to how each hire affects the overall age composition of teams and departments. This leads to age clustering—teams that skew heavily toward one generation—which limits the cognitive diversity and knowledge transfer benefits we've discussed.

Generationally intelligent organizations take a portfolio approach to hiring. When filling a position, they consider not just the individual role requirements but how the hire affects team composition. If a team is heavily weighted toward early-career employees, they might prioritize candidates with more experience. If a team is aging and approaching retirement, they might prioritize younger candidates who can learn from senior team members before they leave.

This doesn't mean age-based hiring decisions, which would be both illegal and counterproductive. It means considering team composition as one factor in hiring decisions, alongside skills, experience, and cultural fit. When you have two equally qualified candidates and one would improve team age diversity while the other would increase age clustering, the diversity consideration can be a tiebreaker.

It also means actively recruiting across age groups rather than relying on recruitment channels that skew toward particular generations. If you recruit primarily through university partnerships, you'll get mostly young candidates. If you recruit primarily through industry conferences and professional networks, you'll get mostly mid-career and senior candidates. Generationally intelligent organizations use diverse recruitment channels to ensure they're reaching candidates across the age spectrum.

Design team composition intentionally. Don't let team composition happen by accident. When forming project teams, task forces, or permanent work groups, explicitly consider age diversity as one dimension of team design.

The goal isn't perfect age balance—that's neither necessary nor always possible. The goal is ensuring that each generation has enough representation that no one feels like a token and that the team can benefit from diverse perspectives. As a rough guideline, aim for at least 20-30% representation from each generation present in your workforce. This provides enough critical mass that people feel comfortable contributing their perspectives.

Also consider the nature of the work when designing teams. For innovation-focused projects, maximize age diversity to get the broadest range of perspectives and approaches. For execution-focused projects, you might prioritize experience and stability. For knowledge-transfer projects, explicitly pair senior employees approaching retirement with junior employees who will carry forward their expertise.

Make team composition decisions transparent. When people understand why teams are structured the way they are, they're more likely to embrace the composition and work effectively within it. If you're pairing a junior employee with a senior employee specifically to facilitate knowledge transfer, tell them that's the goal. If you're creating an age-diverse innovation team to maximize cognitive diversity, explain that rationale.

Develop leaders who can facilitate multi-generational collaboration. Leading multi-generational teams requires different skills than leading age-homogeneous teams. Leaders need to understand generational differences without stereotyping, facilitate communication across different styles, and create environments where all voices are heard.

Invest in leadership development that builds these capabilities. Train leaders to recognize and address generational dynamics. Teach them facilitation techniques that ensure diverse perspectives are integrated. Help them understand their own generational biases and how these might affect their leadership.

Also develop leaders from multiple generations. Don't assume that leadership is only for mid-career and senior employees. Identify and develop high-potential employees across all age groups, creating leadership pipelines that span generations. When younger employees see people from their generation in leadership roles, they're more likely to envision long-term futures with the organization. When older employees see that experience is valued in leadership, they're more likely to stay engaged.

Create structured mentorship programs. Don't rely on informal mentorship to happen organically. While organic mentorship is valuable, structured programs ensure that mentorship opportunities are available to everyone, not just those who are naturally good at building relationships or who happen to work near senior employees.

Implement both traditional mentorship—where senior employees mentor junior employees—and reverse mentorship—where junior employees mentor senior employees on new technologies, trends, and perspectives. Make participation in mentorship programs a valued part of career development for both mentors and mentees.

Set clear expectations and provide training for both mentors and mentees. Mentorship is a skill that can be learned and improved. Don't assume that senior employees automatically know how to mentor effectively or that junior employees know how to make the most of mentorship relationships.

Track and measure mentorship outcomes. Are mentees developing faster? Are mentors staying engaged? Are mentorship relationships leading to better retention? Use this data to continuously improve your mentorship programs.

Implement collaboration tools and processes that work across generations. Technology can either facilitate or hinder cross-generational collaboration, depending on how it's implemented.

When selecting collaboration tools, involve representatives from all generations in the decision-making process. What seems intuitive to a 25-year-old might be confusing to a 55-year-old, and vice versa. Choose tools that are accessible to users with varying levels of technical sophistication, and provide training and support to ensure everyone can use them effectively.

Also maintain multiple communication channels rather than forcing everyone onto a single platform. Some people work better with email, others with instant messaging, others with face-to-face conversation. Create norms about which channels are appropriate for which purposes, but allow flexibility in how people communicate day-to-day.

Implement collaboration processes that ensure all voices are heard. Use techniques like round-robin discussions, anonymous input collection, and structured brainstorming that prevent dominant voices from overwhelming others. These processes are particularly important in multi-generational teams where hierarchical dynamics might otherwise silence junior employees.

Build a culture that values all generations. Culture change is hard and slow, but it's essential for sustainable success with multi-generational teams. You need to create an environment where age diversity is seen as an asset, where stereotypes are challenged, and where people are valued for their contributions regardless of age.

This starts with leadership behavior. When senior leaders visibly value and seek input from employees across all generations, they signal that age diversity matters. When they challenge age-based stereotypes and assumptions, they create permission for others to do the same. When they recognize and reward cross-generational collaboration, they reinforce the behaviors you want to see.

It also requires addressing ageism in both directions—both the stereotyping of older workers as out-of-touch and resistant to change, and the stereotyping of younger workers as entitled and lacking work ethic. These stereotypes are pervasive in many organizations, and they undermine the trust and respect necessary for effective collaboration.

Create opportunities for cross-generational interaction beyond work tasks. Social events, volunteer activities, and informal gatherings help people see each other as individuals rather than generational representatives. When you know someone personally, you're less likely to stereotype them based on age.

Measure and track generational diversity metrics. What gets measured gets managed. Track the age composition of your workforce, teams, and leadership. Monitor engagement and retention across age groups. Measure the outcomes of multi-generational teams compared to age-homogeneous teams.

Use this data to identify problems and opportunities. If you notice that certain departments or teams are heavily age-clustered, investigate why and take corrective action. If you see retention problems in particular age groups, dig into the causes and address them. If multi-generational teams are outperforming homogeneous teams, document and share these successes to build support for generational diversity initiatives.

Also track leading indicators, not just lagging indicators. Don't wait until you have a retention crisis to realize you have a problem. Monitor engagement scores, mentorship participation rates, and team composition metrics that can alert you to issues before they become crises.

Address work style and policy differences. Different generations often have different preferences around work arrangements, communication styles, and career development. Rather than forcing everyone into a single model, create flexibility that accommodates different preferences while maintaining team effectiveness.

This might mean offering flexible work arrangements that allow people to work when and where they're most productive. It might mean providing multiple career paths—not everyone wants to move into management, and not everyone wants to stay in individual contributor roles forever. It might mean offering different types of development opportunities—some people want formal training, others want stretch assignments, others want mentorship.

The key is creating systems that are flexible enough to accommodate different preferences while maintaining fairness and consistency. You can't give everyone exactly what they want, but you can create options that work for different people at different career stages.

Invest in continuous learning and development. In a rapidly changing business environment, everyone needs to keep learning regardless of age. Create a culture of continuous learning where development is expected and supported for all employees.

This means providing learning opportunities that are accessible and relevant to people at different career stages. Junior employees might need technical skills and foundational business knowledge. Mid-career employees might need leadership development and strategic thinking skills. Senior employees might need updates on new technologies and emerging trends.

It also means challenging the assumption that learning and development are only for early-career employees. When you invest in developing senior employees, you signal that they're valued and that you expect them to continue contributing. This improves engagement and retention while keeping your workforce current and capable.

Create succession planning processes that leverage generational diversity. Don't wait until someone announces retirement to think about succession. Build succession planning into your ongoing talent management processes, identifying potential successors early and creating development plans that prepare them for future roles.

Use multi-generational teams as succession planning tools. When you pair potential successors with current role holders for extended periods, succession becomes smooth and natural. The successor learns not just the technical requirements of the role but the relationships, context, and judgment required for success.

Also create succession plans that span multiple generations. Don't assume that the person who will eventually fill a senior role is currently in the next level down. Sometimes the best successor is someone earlier in their career who needs several years of development. By identifying these people early and creating development plans that span years, you build deeper leadership pipelines.

Celebrate and communicate successes. When multi-generational teams achieve great outcomes, make sure people know about it. Share success stories that highlight how generational diversity contributed to results. Recognize and reward individuals and teams that exemplify effective cross-generational collaboration.

This serves multiple purposes. It reinforces the behaviors you want to see. It builds support for generational diversity initiatives by demonstrating their value. It provides role models and examples that other teams can learn from. And it creates positive momentum that makes cultural change easier.

Be patient and persistent. Building a generationally intelligent organization doesn't happen overnight. It requires sustained commitment, continuous improvement, and willingness to learn from both successes and failures.

You'll encounter resistance—from people who are comfortable with age-homogeneous teams, from people who hold generational stereotypes, from people who don't see why this matters. Address this resistance through education, demonstration of results, and persistent leadership commitment.

You'll also make mistakes—team compositions that don't work, mentorship pairings that fail, policies that have unintended consequences. Learn from these mistakes, adjust your approach, and keep moving forward.

The organizations that succeed are those that treat generational diversity as a long-term strategic priority rather than a short-term initiative. They build it into their talent management systems, their leadership development programs, their team design processes, and their cultural norms. They measure progress, celebrate successes, and continuously improve.

And over time, they build sustainable competitive advantages that compound—advantages in innovation, in retention, in engagement, in adaptability, and in organizational resilience. They become the kind of organizations that don't just survive disruption but thrive through it, because they've built the human capital systems and cultural capabilities that enable continuous learning, adaptation, and improvement.

This is what generationally intelligent organizations look like. This is what's possible when you move beyond treating age diversity as a demographic fact and start leveraging it as a strategic asset.

The question isn't whether this approach works—the evidence is clear that it does. The question is whether your organization will embrace it, implement it, and reap the benefits, or whether you'll continue treating generational diversity as a challenge to be managed rather than an opportunity to be seized.

The choice is yours. But the competitive landscape is unforgiving, and the organizations that figure this out first will pull away from those that don't. The window for strategic advantage is open now. How long it stays open depends on how quickly your competitors recognize what you've just learned.

The future belongs to organizations that can harness the full potential of their multi-generational workforces. The future belongs to generationally intelligent organizations.

Will yours be one of them?

10

Bibliography

1. Edmondson, A. C. (2018). *The fearless organization: Creating psychological safety in the workplace for learning, innovation, and growth*. Wiley.
2. Page, S. E. (2007). *The difference: How the power of diversity creates better groups, firms, schools, and societies*. Princeton University Press.
3. Grant, A. (2013). *Give and take: Why helping others drives our success*. Viking.
4. Pink, D. H. (2009). *Drive: The surprising truth about what motivates us*. Riverhead Books.
5. Katzenbach, J. R., & Smith, D. K. (1993). *The wisdom of teams: Creating the high-performance organization*. Harvard Business School Press.

9 789358 122527

Printed at Repro India Ltd.